P9-EIF-171

12932

819.754 Wicks, Ben.
Wicks   Ben Wicks' Canada.   Toronto, McClelland
             and Stewart, 1976.
                125 p.   illus.

         1. Canadian wit and humor.   .I. Title.
         077108983X   0109525

                                           6/cn

Ben Wicks' Canada

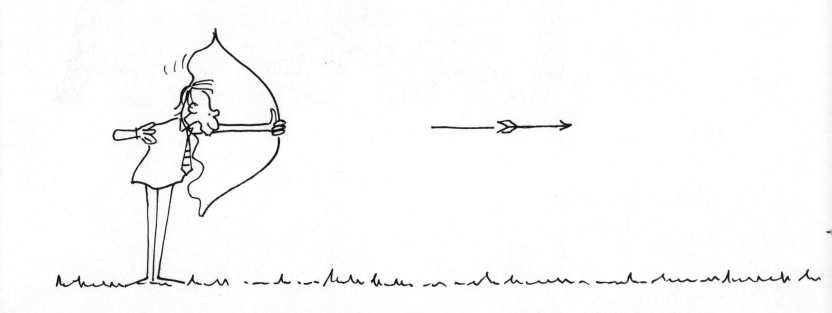

Ben Wicks' CANADA

by Ben Wicks

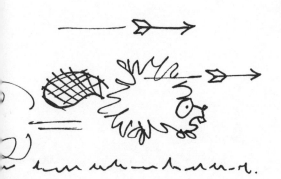

McCLELLAND AND STEWART

0-7710-8983-X

The Canadian Publishers
McClelland and Stewart Limited
25 Hollinger Road
Toronto, Ontario

Printed and bound in Canada

To Doreen

Contents

Acknowledgements

I wish to thank the following.
Without their help it would
have been impossible to put together
this incredibly valuable document:

Sir Frederick Howes

Lord Charmley of Charmal

Sir Kenneth Johnson

Sir Reginald Dibs

Sir Henry Claremont

None of the above have ever been to Canada.
They have, however, seen the movie,
"When I'm calling you" starring Nelson Eddy
and know the subject backwards.

Ben Wicks
Toronto, 1976

Introduction

I am an Englishman.
What is an Englishman?
Let me tell you what an Englishman is not.
An Englishman is not a foreigner.
Foreigners are tall, dark, fair, bilingual,
chew gum ... and speak with an accent.
We, the English, are of average height, smoke
a pipe, and go to the best schools – yet remain
impervious to knowledge. We are all truly
gentlemen and enjoy cricket.
We do have our faults, of course; being overly
modest is probably the worst of them.
Other faults? We're no doubt too decent, too
honest, and too kind to the colonies.
Some people may say we no longer rule the
world.
The point is that the English have the breeding
that *suggests* they rule the world.
Who cares who actually rules it?

Hoping to be seen in the company of an English gentleman, Canadian actor Christopher Plummer tries to fool Wicks by wearing a beard and speaking with an English accent. Mr. Plummer's knowledge of French wines was his undoing. Asked by the ever-wary Wicks as to why he had neglected to order an English draft beer the actor's only reply was "O Merde!"

You may feel I'm being prejudiced.
Rubbish!
Of all the colonies Canada remains my favourite.
Of all the foreigners, Canadians are the ones
I'd choose to sit with on a bus.
So what?
So this!
The country I love is in trouble.
Canada is going to the dogs.
Crime is up.
Church is down.
Porno is 'in'.
Virginity is 'out'.
Births are dropping like flies hit by DDT
as the abortionists knock out their daily dozen.

What is being done about these problems?
Sweet fanny adams!
Canadians feel that this is the way of the world.
"Everyone has problems," they say.
But everyone does *not* have problems.
England does not have problems.

Why?

The inhabitants.

A land filled with people proud of their heritage.
People of vision, culture, substance and distinction.

So what can Canadians do about their problems?
Nothing!
What can I do?
Plenty.
The fact that I am an Englishman living in Canada has
been useful in the writing of this book. For I have a
detachment that is unclouded by a lot of bullshit
nationalism.
Hence I have no hesitation in recommending the cure for
what ails Canada.
We saturate the country with Englishmen:
Englishmen to guide.
Englishmen to lead.
Englishmen to advise.
Englishmen to overcome the problems now besetting
Canada; to steer her along a road of righteousness to still
waters; and therein to rest for all the world to see, marvel
and emulate.

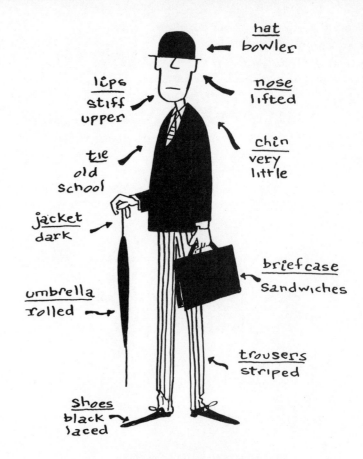

AN ENGLISHMAN

How to recognize an Englishman

Before we get cracking let me make myself quite clear as to the kind of Englishman Canada so desperately needs.
Lots of riffraff have settled in Canada since the end of the Second World War and claim to be English.
Fakes!
These are working-class, lower-class or second-class Englishmen.
To attract more of these will put us in one hell of a pickle.
They breed like bloody rabbits.
In the time it takes you or I to kiss a lady's hand they've got her on her back with her knickers down and are going at it like there's no tomorrow.

UPPER   LOWER

What we need is the "Upper" class.
How can you tell who is "Upper" and who is "Lower"?
Fortunately for us the aristocratic Englishman carries his badge of office with him.

His accent

Of all the foreign dialects the one known as English remains the accepted champion.
Why is it that the English accent remains the envy of the world?
Many foreigners feel that the receding chin enables the English to speak the way they do.
Not so.
The highly developed English tone, that can command the peasantry of the globe to satisfy an Englishman's every whim, is the result of a perfect glottis.
What is a glottis and where is it found?
It lies at the back of the tongue and straight south as the germ flies.
There, in the centre of the windpipe, sits a voice box.
Inside this box sits the glottis.

11

It is in fact a voice production space. A means of producing sound.

Incredible as it may seem, the English production area differs from every other known species of speaking mammal.

Let us take a close look at the glottis of an Englishman and, for the purpose of this book, that of a Canadian.

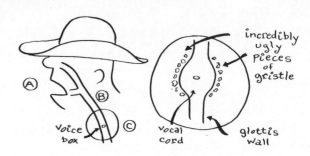

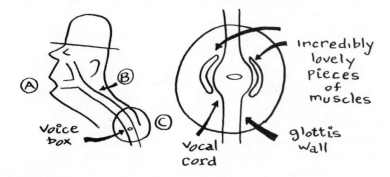

English

The mouth opens (A) and allows air to travel down the windpipe (B) and through the voice box (C). On entering the voice box it begins to gently ease its way around the vocal cord. As it does so, smooth, incredibly lovely pieces of muscle softly push on the glottis walls. This causes the air to pant with pleasure as it continues on its way and in so doing produces the angelic sound known as English.

Canadian

The mouth opens (A) and air wallops its way past a fluoridated tooth and slithers into the windpipe (B). Here it gropes and claws its way to the voice box (C) where rough and incredibly ugly pieces of gristle thump and bang at the glottis walls. This knocks the shit out of the air. Having squeezed its way through, it finally emits a sound that turns and attempts to escape back up the windpipe (D). Finding the mouth closed (E) it then makes for the only exit available, the nose (F). Here it takes on the nasal quality so apparent in the North American accent.

The receding chin

Long ago Englishmen found the action of relieving himself
nauseating, and learned to control the urge.

Of all the virtues bestowed on an Englishman surely this
control is the most envied.

Medical science has attributed this phenomenon to a
hardening of the perineal area.

The art of encouraging this "holding back" can be traced to
the Middle Ages.

Constantly leaving their castle to
give assistance to some poor
unfortunates at home or abroad
these gallant gentlemen would
dress themselves in armour and
gallop off into the sunset.
Fearing that the use of a toilet
would leave their flanks exposed
to attack (not to mention their
rear or front), the knights
controlled their needs until they
were safely back within the castle
walls.
Unfortunately, this restraint
resulted in certain physical
changes taking place.
With their legs crossed in the
saddle to help control the
bladder, the skin was stretched to
the utmost.

The results of this action began
to show in the face and many
knights were forced to keep the
visor of their helmets down for
fear of ridicule.

NO FLY

Unable to take up any slack, the chin itself began to suffer the pulling action.
It began to recede.
The longer the knight was away from his castle, the more his chin receded.
Many knights returned from the Hundred Year's War with no chin at all.

It was during this war that the cry of "Keep a stiff upper lip!" was first heard.
With little or no chin remaining, the need for a stiffening of the upper lip was essential if the upper half of the face was to keep its God-given English shape.

14

Getting the English to leave

Getting the English "Upper" to leave England

How do we get the English to leave a paradise for a wilderness? It won't be easy.

Despite this obvious problem a group of devoted Englishmen have formed a society to help the less fortunate of the world.

The World aristocratic Immigration and Training Society with headquarters in London has dedicated itself to making the world a better place in which to live for all foreigners. I have been given the honour to serve as director of TWITS Canada.

As such it has been my thankless task to cross this vast country and report my findings forthwith.

Pierre Elliott Trudeau listens intently as Wicks explains England's position. "There are just not enough English gentlemen to go around," the immensely likable author told the Prime Minister of Canada.

The Prime Minister shows his pleasure at being told that Quebec will get the pick of the second quota of English arrivals. In return, Mr. Trudeau promised Wicks that the province will be happy to speak English at all times and to give up the French language.

THE ENGLISH ARE COMING!

YIPPEE!

At this news, many Canadians have no doubt begun to cheer.

Aware of the problems that exist in Canada they will rejoice at such swift and special treatment.

I must warn you before you dance around the room that, as yet, victory is not ours.

We have just begun.

The road to our first Englishman will be long and hard.

I have completed my report and it now remains for me to take it to headquarters.

It is not pretty reading.

But take heart. Neither was the Bangladesh report.

17

What are Canada's chances?

Good!

Being a member of the colonies helps, and in this regard Canada is by far the most fortunate beginning as she does with the letter "C".

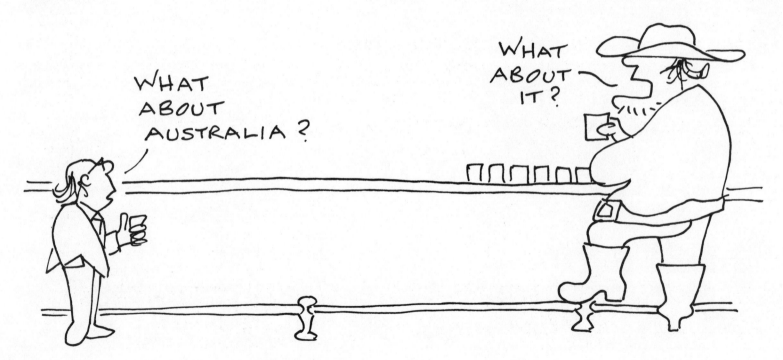

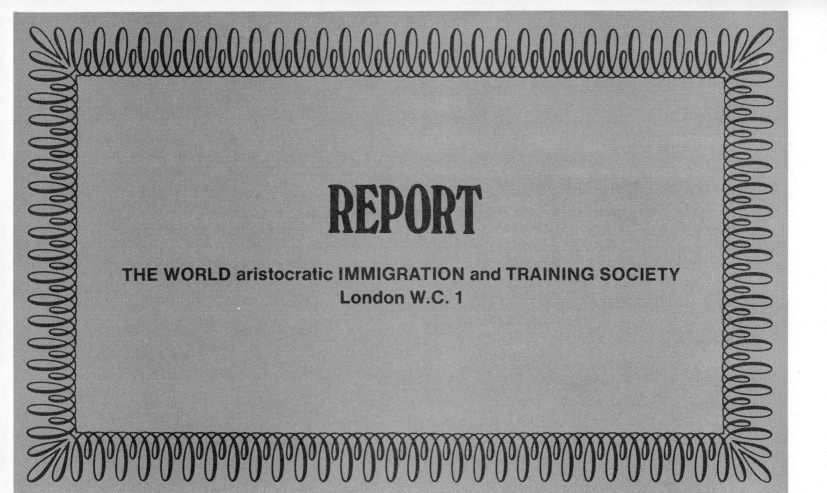

REPORT

THE WORLD aristocratic IMMIGRATION and TRAINING SOCIETY
London W.C. 1

COUNTRY:	Canada
NUMBER OF ENGLISHMEN NEEDED:	A hell-of-a-lot
PURPOSE OF REQUEST:	Breeding
WHERE IS CANADA?	

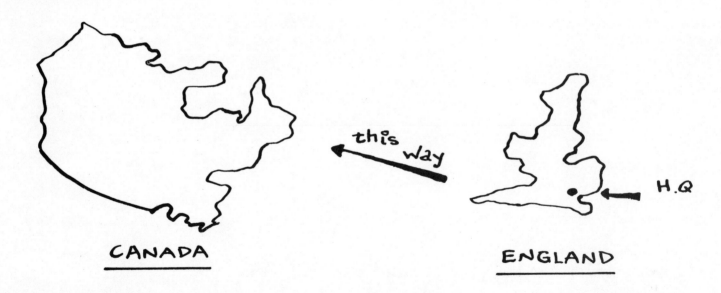

CANADA

this way

H.Q

ENGLAND

How to travel to Canada

There are three ways.
Land, air, or sea.
Should you use the first, travel light.
Go straight up the mall from headquarters, turn right at the
Palace and on into Henley.
Keep straight on and cross the border into Wales.
Past the singing miners at the mine head and turn left at the
old lady sitting by her spinning wheel.
You are now on the beach.

To continue to walk can be a little tricky.
Be prepared for a soggy boot and wet tootsies.
Canada is to the west.

From this point on the only chaps you are likely to meet will be those bloody Irish fellows.
I would avoid speaking to them.
But if you are lost you may have to.
On hearing your English accent it's quite possible they will answer, "Up my arse!"
It's their quaint way of greeting the English.
By any stretch of the imagination, this is not the way to Canada:
I would advise against walking.

FOREIGN STEWARDESS

ENGLISH STEWARDESS

By air
There is only one airline.
British Airways.
With its pie-and-eels and bangers-and-mash it remains by far the cuisine leader of the airways.
You will find that the stewardesses (unlike those on Canadian airlines) will not attempt to make it with the passenger next to you, and will certainly refrain from sticking their tits in your ear every time your neighbour asks for a pillow.

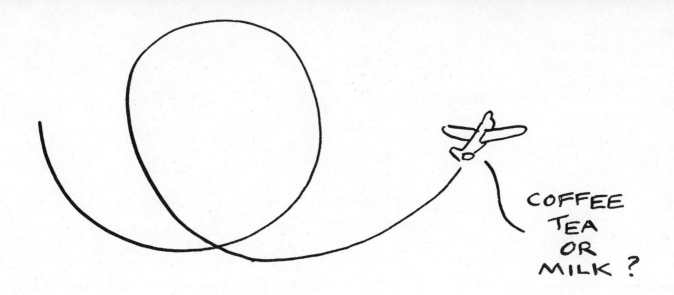

COFFEE
TEA
OR
MILK ?

The pilots are the same ones who shot the hell-out-of-the-hun in two world wars. For a small fee he'll be happy to perform a roll with a spin off the top just as coffee is being served to an "Upper Canada" bore that you've been stuck with as a seat companion.

The fare will be the same as that charged by all airlines crossing the Atlantic.

Exorbitant.

By boat

To choose an English ship when crossing the Atlantic is to multiply your chances of getting a hell-of-a-dunking at the first sign of floating ice.

For reasons completely beyond me English ocean-going liners just can't resist the stuff.

Because of this obvious drawback I would suggest that you book your passage on a Canadian ship.

Since the ship is foreign the chances of it finding a watery grave are about 50-50.

At the first sign of trouble make for the best-looking row-boat.

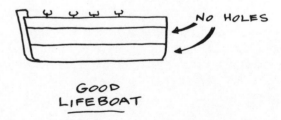

Being a Canadian ship out of Europe, the atmosphere on board will be chaotic.

Many of the screaming mass throwing themselves to one knee on the deck will be European emigrants.

Since this action is occurring on the side of the ship nearest the waves the chances of the ship turning over are greatly enhanced.

There is no time to lose.

By now others will be attempting to join you in the lifeboat. Be selective.

Remember that this is the kind of vessel that requires hefty arms to propel it through the water.

Not the kind of arms usually found connected to the bodies of women and children.

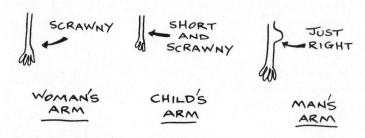

Suggest to any woman or child approaching your boat that you are full up.

They will no doubt point out that you are sitting in an empty boat.

Show them the ugly end of a boat hook and repeat "full up!"

If they still fail to understand repeat the action with the boat hook and scream in their ear "F - - - OFF!"

This usually has the desired effect.

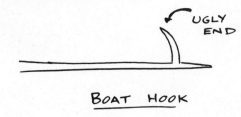

At this point there will probably
be some light relief.
Your captain will no doubt
inform you that he has decided to
go down with the ship.
Try not to smile.
This can be very funny and, let's
face it, will mean an extra seat in
the boat for your feet.

Fun and games aboard a foreign ship

*The winners of the final night fancy dress contest line the rails and wait for
the captain to give them their prizes.*
Mercifully a ship close by was able to save most of them from the icy waters.

26

Once you have the necessary number of arms in your boat start rowing from the disaster area pronto.

Get a sing-song going.

This lifts the spirits of those in the boat and has the added advantage of drowning out the sounds of those poor sods that remain in the water.

If you are having difficulty getting away from survivors you are doing something wrong in the rowing department.

The best results are obtained by placing an equal number of oars (the long wooden things) on each side of the boat.

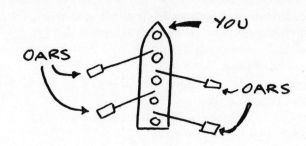

BOAT
BIRDS-EYE VIEW

Once the oars are in the water each man should pull on them.

If this doesn't move the boat check to see that each man is pulling in the same direction.

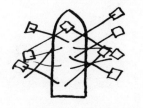

WRONG

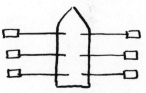

RIGHT

27

Survivors of past ship-wrecks have mentioned seeing the captain actually go down with the ship. Now this can be great fun, and is obviously a sight most of those in the boat will not want to miss.

Just remember that it is not wise for everyone to jump up in the boat at the same time.

At the cry of "There he goes!" you may very well find yourselves keeping him company.

Eventually you will be rescued.

When the rescue ship arrives it's considered good form to ask that the others in the boat, regardless of their colour or country of origin, be rescued at the same time as yourself.

Whatever happens and God willing, you will eventually land in Canada.

Canada's provinces

Newfoundland

The first piece of Canada sighted, it remains the closest of all the Canadian provinces to England.

Jealous at being so much farther from the seat of learning than the Newfoundlander, the rest of Canada direct scorn and abuse at the people of the island by making them the brunt of a series of humorous stories called "Newfy" jokes.

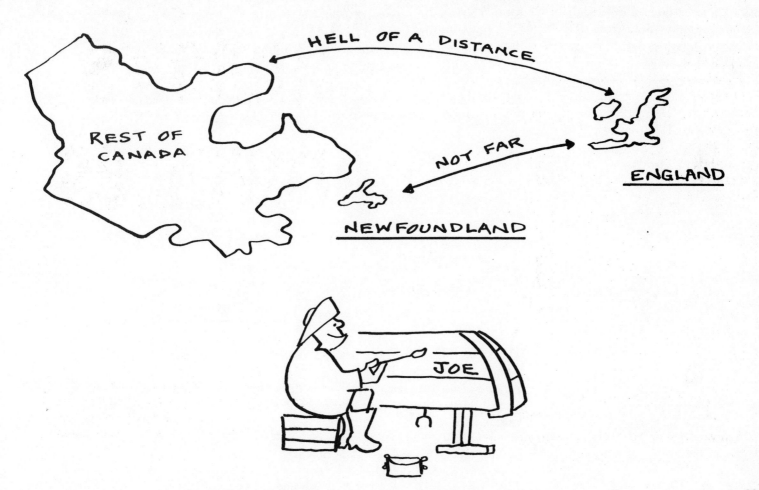

By a quirk of fate, to approach Newfoundland from the west is to mistakenly feel that the island is indeed England.

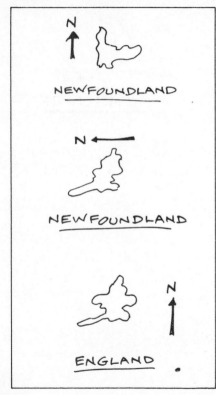

Many Canadian tourists travelling by charter flights to London have been flown to the island and feel to this day that they have spent two weeks in England. By continuing this myth, Newfoundland is able to supplement its meagre fishing industry with a growing, if disappointed, number of tourists.

The island is ruled by King Joseph the First of Smallwood, whose twin brother, Prince Jean of Drapeau, rules the principality of Montreal.

The Prime Minister of the island is an extremely good-looking young man named Gordon Pinsent.

He loves Newfoundland dearly and does everything in his power to spread the word of how glorious it is to live on an island covered in fishing huts.

Mr. Pinsent makes his home in Toronto.

I myself have never been to the island but from various sightings reported to me I have compiled the following drawing:

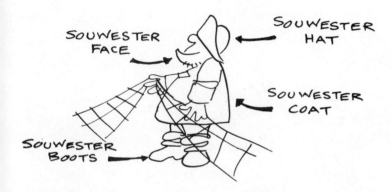

SOUWESTER FACE

SOUWESTER HAT

SOUWESTER COAT

SOUWESTER BOOTS

Nova Scotia

To the south of Newfoundland lies Nova Scotia.
It was the first province in Canada to have a distillery.
Not surprisingly such an attraction has encouraged people of all races to make this part of Canada their home; Germans, French, Negroes, Irish, Scots: all of these are to be found in Nova Scotia.
Hardly the kind of area to be recommended for English settlers. ...

Prince Edward Island

P.E.I., as it is so fondly called by the people of Canada, is the smallest of the provinces.

AN ANT

PRINCE EDWARD ISLAND

It is completely surrounded by water making it extremely difficult to find a place to sit for the 110,000 Canadians who stand on the island.

WHAT TIME IS THE NEXT FERRY?

YOU'RE STANDING ON MY TOE!

STOP THAT, I'M A MARRIED MAN!

The island's greatest achievement was to find sufficient chairs for a group of politicians who met on the island and decided to call Canada a country.

This brilliant evaluation by a group of seated men has prompted many members of the island community to demand a chair for all those living on the island.

Such a manoeuvre would hopefully result in PEI giving up its title as the most boring place in Canada to grow potatoes.

Sir John A. Macdonald rises to offer his seat to a late-comer. The eight standing members immediately demanded to know why, since he is late, he should be offered a seat while they must stand. "Because," answered Sir John, "he has no feet!" Despite this answer, one member of the group (left of centre) makes a paper spear with which to catch Sir John a swift smack in the earhole the moment the Canadian Prime Minister's back is turned.

Quebec

Nowhere in Canada is it more apparent that you are in a foreign country than it is in Quebec. For one thing, the language is close to that of the French language. This is not surprising when we discover that it was indeed the French who first settled in this neck of the woods. Unfortunately (for the French), the new arrivals had no sooner put their feet up than an English chap by the name of Wolfe turned up and told them that the part of Canada they had decided to call home did in fact belong to England.

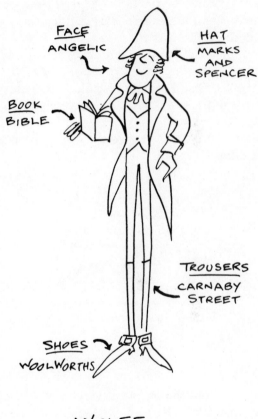

FACE
ANGELIC

HAT
MARKS
AND
SPENCER

BOOK
BIBLE

TROUSERS
CARNABY
STREET

SHOES
WOOLWORTHS

WOLFE

Why this should be the case I haven't the foggiest idea but feel that if an Englishman were making the statement it would no doubt be true.

The French, led by an incredibly brutal and barbaric man called Montcalm, refused to budge.

"For the last time I'm telling ye olde Frenchie to pack your bags – and piss offe," said the extremely likable and kindly Wolfe.

"But I was here first," replied the ill-disposed, truculent Montcalm.

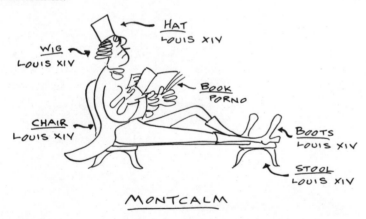

MONTCALM

"We'll see about thatie," said the gracious, amiable and obliging Wolfe as he made his way down a steep cliff to gather an army. Boarding his ship he gathered his five million Englishmen around him and told them the news.

"We've got this foreign chappie at the top of yonder cliffe, lads, who says that all Englishmen are a lot of fayries who can't fight for toffee."

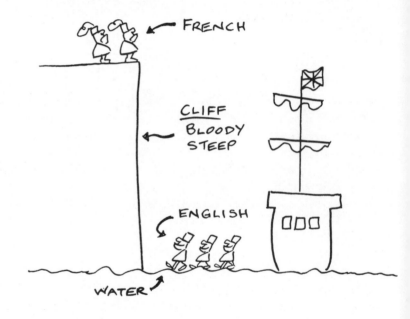

BATTLE OF THE PLAINS

Although many were in fact "fayries", no one likes to be called a coward. So they followed Wolfe up the cliff and met the French on a flat piece of ground called the Plains of Abraham.

It was all over in a matter of hours.

The pistol-packing French were no match for five million screaming, scratching, hanky-waving troops.

ENGLISH SOLDIER

The tender, benevolent, fond, charitable Wolfe died during the punch-up but not before the savage, cold-blooded, pitiless, ruthless Montcalm had bit the dust.

The French Canadian is a very bitter fellow.

He suffered defeat at the hands of the British many years ago and to this day feels that he is a prisoner in his own country.

Quebec calls itself "la belle province" which I'm told in translation means that it is a beautiful province.

It is.

But considering its past behaviour toward the English it's not to be recommended as a settlement area.

What's more, the weather is colder than hell.

Not, however cold enough for the average Canadian.

He needs it colder.

How else can he boast of his ability to suffer the most extreme of weathers?

He is brainwashed at an early age into subtracting 25 degrees from the lowest of temperature readings.

"There was a young lad from Quebec
Who stood in the snow to his neck
When asked "Are you friz?"
He replied "Yes I is,
But we don't call this cold in Quebec."

Ontario

To arrive in Ontario is to arrive in a province that offers the ideal prerequisite for a settling Englishman.
A means of escape.
No province is better equipped to escape from.
There are 85,000 miles of roads and wonderful airline facilities.

For this reason, one in every three Canadians lives in the province.
Many of these are English (lower-class) and Italian.
For the Italian, anything is better than living in Europe – naturally.
Most of them have their passport stamped and race for the nearest construction sites.
These sites are to be found in Toronto.

Toronto

Under the nimble, raucous hands of these men of Napoli, buildings have sprung up like a bunch of dandelions on a suburban lawn.

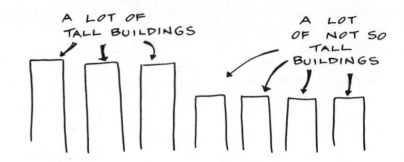

Naturally this has not pleased everyone.
Certainly the Mayor of Toronto was depressed to find himself surrounded by tall structures.
This is understandable.
He is 5ft. 6in. in height.
The decision to make a home for the tallest tower in the world in the city of Toronto was the last straw.
"That's it!" said the mayor. "I've had it up to here with buildings."
His hand was levelled at his throat.

So a height regulation was set at five feet.
No building in the city would be allowed to exceed this height.
This of course did not please everyone.
Particularly builders of elevators!
However, a mayor in Canada commands respect.

RESPECT

Has this ruling been good for Toronto?
Yes and no.
On-site construction accident figures are way down, and much of the credit for this should be given to the mayor's ruling.

Accidents have all but been eliminated as workers hook their safety belts to scaffolding four feet above the city. Unfortunately falling hammers continue to take their toll. Removing his helmet to wipe the sweat from his brow, Mario Anglino, a two-foot midget, was struck by a hammer that fell from the sixth floor, three feet from the ground.
"How was I to know that the little runt was walking under me?" said his likable foreman, Harry Conkin, at the funeral of Mario a few days later.

Displaying the ready wit and brilliant repartee with which the English are noted, the author donned the clothes of a Northern Ontario inhabitant much to the delight of Everest climber, Sir Edmund Hillary.

Ottawa

Anyone rushing to get out of Toronto may make the major mistake of smacking head-on into the town of Ottawa.

What's wrong with Ottawa?

It's full of civil servants.

Worse, it's full of Canadian civil servants.

It is the home of the Prime Minister and Governor-General of Canada.

This order of listing in no way supercedes the fact that the Queen is in charge and makes an occasional visit.

Rather than spend the time in lavish praise of Her Majesty let us bash right on and cover the area of "who runs the country?"

Ottawa is the captain's bridge of Canada.

There are three major parties.
The team at bat at the moment is
a group of fellows called
Liberals.
A bunch of nignogs calling
themselves Conservatives are
fielding and someone called NDP
sits in the stands.

The games are all played in
Ottawa and consist of a lot of
talk and very little action.
Most of the chat is to enable
members of each team, through
reports in their local newspapers,
to prove to their voters that they
are still alive if not omnipotent.

Niagara Falls remains one of the most famous of all honeymoon locations.
Pictures, such as this one, have done much to publicize the small Ontario town. Jean Hammond, daughter of the Rev. Ian Hammond, is seen here with her new husband, the Rev. Victor Price. Anxious to get away from the crowds that gathered at the church the newly married couple found an ideal hiding place and were last seen heading down stream toward Horseshoe Falls. We wish them every success.

Stratford

The small town of Stratford in Ontario commands a place in the hearts of most Canadians. Here during the summer months the impression is given that Shakespearean plays are being performed.
Powerful actors like Henry Ascort can be seen alongside international stars.

Ascort, the winner of many honors for acting, is seen here at the annual "Ship's Wheel" awards for one-legged actors. Accepting the "Wheel" as best peg-legged actor of the year, Ascort turned and thanked his producer Flora Hennessy for her unflagging devotion during the making of "These Boots Were Made For Walking". Unaware that his wooden leg was on her foot, Ascort continued with his acceptance speech for an hour-and-a-half, as Flora fought back what many thought were tears of gratitude.

Manitoba

We are now at the Manitoba border.
The Prairies lie ahead.
A new world is about to open – a world of wheat,
and more wheat!

Who eats all this wheat?
The Chinese.
Once a people who would rather eat rice than have sex,
they suddenly found themselves unable to resist the
pressure-selling of Canada's Prime Minister.
Disguised as a Chinaman (he has the same shape of eyes),
he infiltrated the country before the "Hoover" salesman
could get a look-in.
Unconfirmed reports tell of Mr. Trudeau walking the
Chinese wall dressed as a mandarin with a satchel full of
wheat samples.

On being questioned, the Prime Minister confessed that he did indeed walk along the wall, but denied that he was carrying wheat.

"All I had in my case were seven fishes and one loaf of bread."

Whatever it was he took with him, the Chinese were impressed.

MILLIONS OF CHINESE (SMILING)

Anxious for rain, a Manitoba farmer stands by as Wicks tries the newest English rain-making device, a striped board banged together to the tune of "Rule Britannia." Worried that Wicks was in Manitoba to take the World Pumpkin Growing Championship from him, the Canadian farmer was soon put at ease.

"The English do not break records," said the genial Wicks, "they make them."

Four hundred million people switched overnight from rice crispies to wheatie bits.

Did this make the prairie farmer happy?

It did not.

Before this globe-trotting leader began meddling, the Canadian farmer had spent his time down on the farm safe in the knowledge that the government was paying him to hang around and just grow as much of the golden stuff as he could. Not for him the worry of selling wheat.

"Just grow it. We'll get rid of it somehow," he was told.

Now the government has found someone who wants it.
A way of getting their money back.
Filthy loot has raised its ugly head.
No longer will the farmer get the tractor from the shed to take him to the bank for his government cheque.
Now he has to ride it in the fields.
The government has now found a ready answer to the voters' cry of
"What the hell is going on up in Ottawa?"
Now they can snap back: "Don't bother us, we're busy selling wheat to the Chinese."
Seven hundred million people wanted four sandwiches each for their daily lunch bucket, and the government was ready to prod the prairie farmers into getting it for them.
This made the prairie farmer very unhappy.
Now besides growing the stuff he was expected to cut the wheat, tie the sheaves, crush the corn, shape the dough, bake the bread, and wrap it before placing each loaf on a train for Vancouver.

← DOUGH

Tractor companies did their best to help out as new machines were developed to handle the job.
Soon giant wrapping and slicing machines could be seen beside the harvesters (see photo).
Farmers' wives worked day and night as each was allotted the task of baking 75,000 loaves of bread per day (6,879 farmers' wives, four sandwiches times 700 million at 13 slices to the loaf). Is it any wonder the Canadian prairie farmer and his family to this day vote Conservative?

A new giant wrapping machine is brought to a halt as the farmers look toward the cameraman in the hope that his help can be recruited once the picture-taking is over.
The pipe to the left of the picture is discarding unwanted breadcrumbs.

Saskatchewan

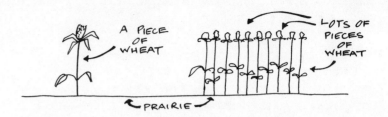

A PIECE OF WHEAT

LOTS OF PIECES OF WHEAT

← PRAIRIE →

Having crossed Manitoba, one has seen enough wheat to last a lifetime.
Well "you ain't seen nothin' yet," as they say in the movies.
You are about to enter Canada's "Breadbasket" – Sask.

Three-fifths of Canada's wheat is grown in this province. Although the northern part is rocky and covered in lakes and forests, the south is as flat as an ironing board that has been hit by a runaway steam roller.

The name Saskatchewan was given to the province by the Cree Indians.
Knowing that the white man was on his way west they figured on a plan to slow him down.

It worked.

Try as they may, the early settlers were unable to say "Saskatchewan."
Without being able to pronounce the name of the place they wanted to go to, they obviously hadn't a hope in hell of ever getting there.
"Excuse me. I wonder if you could direct me to Saskatooner ... or I mean Sachwanooker ... no Saskkawarner ... Sachachooker ...? Which is the way to Toronto?"

Regina

Saskatchewan is the home of the Royal Canadian Mounted Police.
It's one of the most famous police forces in the world and has its headquarters in Regina.
Why Regina?
Because in Regina it's possible to ride a horse in a circle without fear of bumping into another rider.

Day in and day out, 5,000 Mounties leap from their beds, jump on their horses and begin to ride in a circle.
Not just any circle.
A wonderful new circle developed by an RCMP officer, Supt. Tucker. A musical circle.
It was a time of crisis.
Men no longer enjoyed spending valuable police time getting a man for themselves.

Jeannette MacDonald was no longer young enough to satisfy the needs of most new recruits.
Aware that the numbers of the force were sinking to an all-time low, Supt. Tucker took immediate action.
What was needed was a new means of passing the long lonely hours in the saddle.
It was decided to hold dances.
Although Regina is noted for its lovely pieces of crackling, few of them would agree to dance with someone who insisted on remaining seated on a horse.

Obviously it was not possible for the Mounties to dance with each other.
One or the other would have to dismount; an unheard of action for any Mounted Policeman.

THIS DANCE IS TAKEN

The solution was obvious.
The men would dance with the horses.
So began a practice that continues to this day. Horse and rider locked together in a magic world of motion.
In Regina on a Saturday night one can hear the sounds of laughter, happy neighing, and the gentle rhythm of "Who's taking you home tonight?" gently floating across the wheat and vanishing into the distant light of a prairie moon.

Supt. Tucker, seen here with his wife, Beryl (the one on the right).
"Without her help I would never have thought of the idea," said Tucker.
This delightful picture was taken just before Tucker entered the Regina area ballroom championships.
"We would have won," said Tucker, "if my horse had not lost a shoe."

Alberta

Calgary is Alberta.
Oh, I know that the capital of the province is in Edmonton but who the hell wants to go all that way north when you can meet the same kind of people 200 miles to the south.

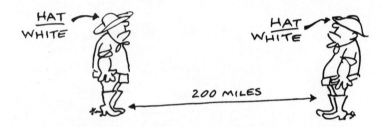

In Calgary you will see a real live cowboy in his regular working clothes: dirty hat, dirty boots, and a dirty shirt. Why is he so dirty?
Regardless of what you may have seen on the screen the job he does is bloody dirty work.

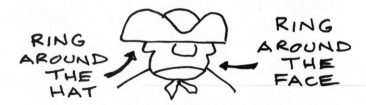

In preparing his report, Wicks visited Calgary. Overcome with excitement at meeting such a distinguished visitor one Calgarian challenged Wicks to a race. Conscious of the man's advancing years, Wicks was seen to lift a finger in a patient gesture before telling the elderly runner that when approaching an Englishman it is customary to speak only when spoken to.

Mind you, once a year he gets away from the grind and attends the famous Calgary stampede.
Here as a change from riding horses and branding cattle he rides horses and brands cattle.
For some strange reason they seem to enjoy doing these things.
A crowd of them get into a set of wagons pulled by horses and go around and around.
I myself felt the whole exercise could be improved considerably if they included hurdle and hedge obstacles.

INJUNS!

Those cowboys that get sick of riding on the inside of a wagon get the chance to ride a horse.
For some reason a horse that stands as quiet as a lamb inside a stall suddenly becomes a raving lunatic the moment a cowboy gets on its back.
Maybe it's got something to do with their genes; the cowboys, that is. I do hear that they are very good lovers.

It gets extremely cold in Alberta.
To keep warm the people of the province dance.
Unable to completely free their joints most dance in a square.

SQUARE DANCERS

For this activity shirts and skirts are worn that are covered in squares in the hopes that those watching become so mesmerized by the patterns that none will notice the dancers' inability to dance in a circle.

The whole procedure is directed by a character called a caller. It's his job to spot those most likely to bash into a fellow dancer, and to direct the fellow about to get clunked into a safe corner.

49

The difficulty of the job of "caller" was appreciated at the 1960 Square Dance finals held in Banff. Unaware that his drink had been spiked, caller Rex Tripper gave a wrong direction and two dancers went out through the barn door and haven't been seen since. Many locals say that if Tripper had given the right calls the same couple would have still gone out the barn door. Not knowing the couple involved I hesitate to make a judgement.

Banff

At the mention of Banff I'm reminded that I have neglected what many people feel is the most beautiful part of Canada. Is it?
There's just a lot of mountains up there.
If you've seen one you've seen them all.
Sure, some are a little more hilly than others but there's nothing that the old Rolls couldn't handle at a pinch.
And speaking of the Rolls –
the province is rolling in loot.
Oil is coming out of their ears.
They have so much of the stuff they don't know what to do with it.

"For god's sake!" cried the Premier, "don't send any more money. I haven't finished counting the last lot." The last lot to which he was referring came in with the 1918 returns.

LOTS OF MONEY → ← PREMIER

Alberta remains the only province in Canada without a sales tax.
The government sits in Edmonton;
so far away from everyone in the province (except those living in Edmonton) that they bother no one.
It all sounds like a paradise; but keep in mind that it's more than 7,000 miles from England.

British Columbia

So bloody wet that to be without an umbrella in Vancouver is to be without your trousers in church. "Come on out," the inhabitants shout, "it's just like England." Just like England, in a pig's ear. It's overrun with Orientals; touches two American states; and has a bunch of leaders hiding out on an island.
And what about the island?
It's named after Queen Victoria and, like her, I was not amused. It's ersatz land.
A copybook world of waxworks, tea shoppes and Anne Hathaway cottages.

To the north of Vancouver lies northern B.C.
Although the area is full of trees and little else, the native people who live and work there are bloody marvellous.

Dressed in lumber jackets and toques (the men), they busy themselves during the day by chopping down any tree that stands in the way of their taking a leisurely stroll through the woods. When it's time for lunch, two or more will band together and clear an area about twenty feet in diameter.
This action is repeated in the evening.
Naturally enough the supper space is a little larger.
This is to accommodate a campfire.
Supper over, the "choppers" gather around and sing songs of the trails they've cut. Many of these campfire melodies have become famous.

One that comes to mind is, of course, "Lilli Marlene."

UNDERNEATH
THE LAMP
LIGHT

I myself was invited to northern B.C. when in Vancouver preparing this report. A particularly lovely area of the forest was giving even the most experienced of lumberjacks problems.

Hearing that an Englishman was a few miles to the south, the King of the forest, Nelson MacEddy, contacted me and asked if I would help out.

Naturally I agreed.

"Your biggest problem is the foot action," I told them.

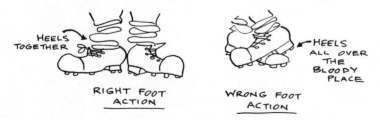

HEELS
TOGETHER

RIGHT FOOT
ACTION

HEELS
ALL OVER
THE
BLOODY
PLACE

WRONG FOOT
ACTION

"It's just a matter of mind over matter," explained Wicks as he cleared an area of particularly bothersome Douglas Fir.

A gushingly grateful MacEddy insisted I stay for the night. It's an evening I shall long recall with affection. The lumberjacks with their toques and checkered shirts and me in my bow-tie and tails sitting cross-legged to eat the evening meal.

As I lay in my sleeping bag (ermine-lined) the sound of a Mountie sleigh drifted through the forest as a French-Canadian fugitive slithered between the moonlit trees. The howl of a lone wolf gently drifted through the whistling trees as I slowly sank into a gratifying stupor and began to dream of Her Majesty.

I DO HOPE IT'S NOT TEA BAGS!

Having arrived at the West Coast
I am suddenly aware that I have
neglected to mention New Brunswick.

New Brunswick.

Northern Territories

Many parts of Canada remain
uninhabited.
Much of this is at the top of the
map.
This is known as the North West
Territories – an ideal name since
most of the land can be found to
the north and slightly west of a
centre line through Canada.
It's full of snow, ice and Eskimo
carvings.
Most Canadians I spoke to felt
that it was by far the most
beautiful part of Canada. ...
There again, most Canadians I
spoke to had never been north of
Winnipeg.

Not wishing to leave a stone
unturned, I took a trip north to
see for myself.
I was not impressed.

To get around can be tricky.
Most of the inhabitants use dogs and
sleighs.
I tried this and was not successful.
For one thing, to get the dogs to stay on
the sleigh can be difficult.

I finally succeeded in moving over the snow with the dogs in tow but despite my repeated shouts of "mush" continued to sink up to my private parts with each trot.

Most Canadians living above the Arctic Circle use the plane like you and I would use a knife and fork.
There are few roads and those that have been built run for three miles before ending at the edge of a frozen lake.
Since they begin at the same spot, to travel by road is not the best way to see the North.

After all is said and done, it boils down to what the woman from London said after her first visit to Scotland:
"Boring. There's nothing but a lot of scenery up there!"

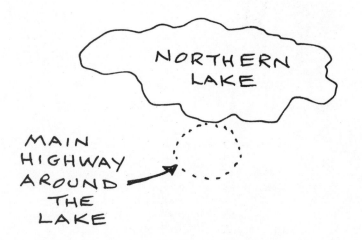

The Yukon

The very name sends chills up the spine of road-builders everywhere.
The Alaska Highway.
This magnificent road originated as an escape route for the many Japanese who had settled in the Vancouver area.

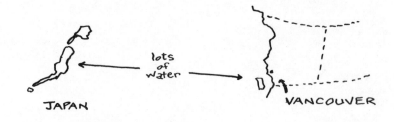

Desperately homesick after fleeing Japan during the China-Japanese war of '37, the small smiling people began to look for some way to get back to their homeland.

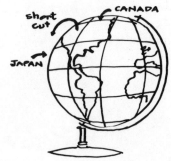

With the little money they had saved during their years in Canada many found it impossible to find the fare required for the long ship ride home.
Obviously the land route was the only answer.
So they began.
Renting cars to cover the trip to Dawson, 150 million Japanese (included in this number are the wives and children) set off on their long journey.

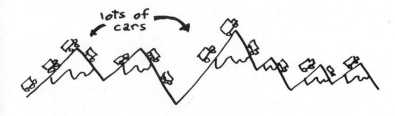

The date, October 1st, 1938. A day now celebrated by Japanese everywhere as Yong Chung Day.
Arriving at the rented car drop-off point in Dawson the 150 million retrieved their deposit and lined up in single file to begin the long trek northward.

The winter was in with a vengeance. Luckily most of them were short, as the picture above shows, and missed the worst of the blowing snow. With the heavy boots all of them were wearing they made short work of the 1,000-mile journey, covering the distance in less than two years.

On reaching Whitehorse they stopped for lunch.

Behind them lay a straight flat line one thousand miles in length.

Now for the first time a road existed where no road had been before.

One hundred and fifty million pairs of boots had torn and cut their way through some of the most desolate country known to man. (Three hundred million individual boots; or 900 million boot studs; or 1,800 million pieces of leather.)

IT'S TWO LANE ALL THE WAY TO DAWSON!

JAPANESE BOOT

JAPANESE BOOT (WITH STUDS)

For their hard work, diligence and loyalty each member of the road-building team was given a little grey home in the West for the duration of the war.

It was as they were sitting eating their lunch that they heard the first news of the war in Europe. The Allies were losing. They were unable to get desperately-needed supplies and the vital link between Paris and Inuvik was in danger of being cut off.

The Japanese hurried to the office of the authorities in Whitehorse and told them of the road they had built. Here was the way to get the desperately-needed supplies to the beleaguered Allied garrisons.

So was born the Alaska Highway.

I believe gold was found somewhere in the Yukon but have had difficulty in finding a record of the happening.

Defending Canada

Canada is the only country in the world that maintains three services under one hat.

Conscious of the incredible increase in the cost of uniforms Canada decided that to be a soldier, sailor or airman does not matter.

The important thing is to be a person who can't wait to get his hands around the neck of anyone who so much as throws a dirty look the way of Canada.

Whether or not the hands belong to someone wearing red, blue or green, is secondary to the fact that the hands are at the end of a sleeve that has "Canada" written across the shoulder flash.

It has had the desired effect. Not one "enemy person"

has set foot on Canada's soil since the Second World War. And even then they were prisoners.

Running in a line from east to west across the top of Canada it has yet to see action.

Should Canadians feel (for whatever reason) that we, the English, are not welcome I am setting out a drawing of the actual defence line with suggested areas of weakness.

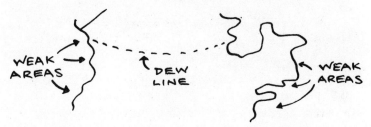

Much of the credit for this must be given to the gallant men who devised a line of defences known as the "Dew" line. Although at first suggestion the plan came under heavy criticism (many thought it to be anti-Semitic), it is now credited with deterring the most ambitious of enemy armies from setting foot on Canadian soil.

Up She Goes

Part of Canada's famous "Dew" line defence system is seen here being modernized and returned to an upright position.

Built to withstand an attack of "Slut-Bug" (the latest in the germ warfare arsenal) it has been heightened. Feeling that the fiendish Slut-Bug could not fly above eight feet, Ottawa defence officials were shocked to learn that during the mating season this height is increased by two feet.

Work began this week to correct this lapse in Canada's northern defences.

This, then, is the country.

What about the natives?

A very mixed bunch

Few countries in the world suffer such a mixed bag of humans. They come in all sizes, shapes and colours.

Is there a typical Canadian?

There is.
He watches from 8 to 29 hours of television a week, and spends an average of 7 hours a week listening to the radio. He shuns an active part in sports and doesn't work on arts and crafts.
The typical Canadian has a 39.3 hour-a-week manufacturing job and is married.
He has 1.7 children; .7 of whom are having their teeth straightened.
He is an overweight, unilingual smoker who is likely to die of circulatory ailments at the age of 69 years and 21 weeks.

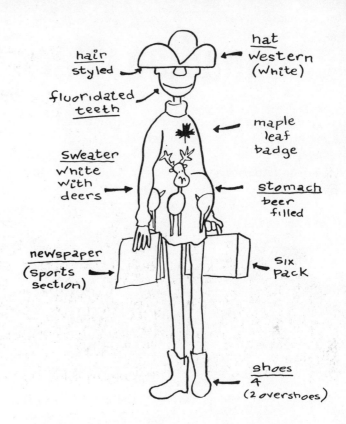

hair styled
hat western (white)
fluoridated teeth
maple leaf badge
sweater white with deers
stomach beer filled
newspaper (sports section)
six pack
shoes 4 (2 overshoes)

TYPICAL CANADIAN

The Canadian male

Loves camping, ice-hockey, woollen sweaters with antelopes-at-play, and weekend cabins.

Anxious to carry the traditions of his pioneer forebears into the twentieth century he throws himself like a madman at jobs around the house.

The volumes of "How To" books pour in as the Canadian male sets about his weekend task.

HOW TO ROB A BANK

His shelves are filled with the incomplete volumes of supermarket handyman books.

Every Canadian has the 'A' and no-one owns the 'B'.

If the wives of the early settlers were to arrive today they would be forced to stand around for years as their husbands busied themselves with the building of an *A*ttic followed by the installation of a *B*ath before he got around to building the *C*abin.

Do they ever progress beyond 'A'?

They certainly do ... 'B'.

B is for Boats

Canadians are intrigued with boats.
Wherever they live they own a boat.
Two thousand miles from the nearest water, there it stands.
A boat.
   Boats on the highway
   Boats in the driveway
   Boats behind cars
   Boats on top of cars
   Occasionally you will find a boat that has made it to
   water!
Canadians feel that this love and possession of boats places
them in a particularly advantageous position in a world
that turns more and more to the ways of EVIL.

LITTLE
BOAT

BIG
BOAT

WATER

Certainly in the second coming of a flood, Canadians will have little to fear from a shortage of arks.

Maybe they feel this makes them the chosen few.

Daily throughout the summer months they flaunt their prowess at walking on water.

There they stand behind their boats and, not content to equal the accomplishments of Christ, surpass his achievements by twisting, turning, and standing on one foot in a religious ritual the likes of which has not been seen since Hannibal carried an elephant across the Alps.

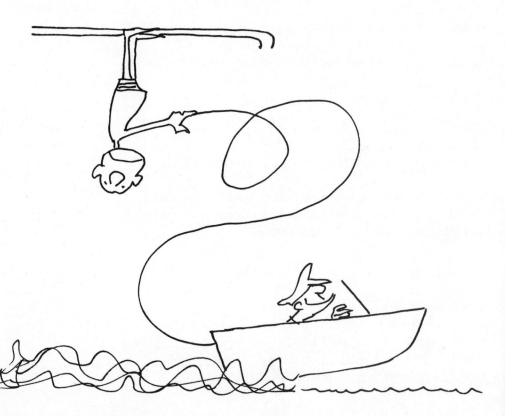

Canadian women

Work, attend cocktail parties, collect monies for symphony orchestras and enter hospital once a year to have their hysterectomy removed.

Once past the age of 25 years they deteriorate rapidly.
I'm told it's the harsh weather.
I'm not surprised.
Although still handsome, I myself have found the odd wrinkle appearing around the eyes.
All are grossly overweight and spend their every waking hour flogging themselves with exercises in a frantic effort to get into a size 10 dress.

Once into her size 10 she decides all is not as it should be.
Her top is too small.
The cure? A bra that crosses the heart.
Her rear sticks out.
The answer? Tight panty hose to pull it in.
She is now
the shape of
an ice-cream cone.
A true Canadian
beauty.

Having set fire to her home, a typical Canadian girl stands anxiously awaiting the arrival of the firemen in the hope that one or more will find her attractive.

Canadian children

They're giants.
The biggest kids the world has ever seen are rolling out of Canadian mothers like ten-ton trucks from G.M.

Desperate to feed these monsters, most mothers wave a white flag on the second day of their life and shove a bottle into their ever-open mouths.

Once off the bottle it's worse.
Jars of apple, meat, pablum, and peaches pack the supermarket shelves in a hopeless attempt to keep up.

When they finally get to the hard stuff, all control is thrown to the wind.

It's a hopeless battle that drives Canadian women from the house in ever-increasing numbers.
Better to be hit by a bus than run down by a hungry dinosaur on its way to the fridge.

Schools

Large buildings that absorb incredible amounts of money in order to prepare Canada's youth for a life of in-activity.

Conscious of the need to keep the pupils from dozing off, the ever-concerned leaders of education have devised a new method of delivering information.
Known by its code name of "New Math" it is completely incomprehensible.
Now teachers and students, far from dozing, spend their days struggling over problems that just a few years back were solved on the fingers of classroom hands.

And what of play?
Gymnasiums the size of football fields and swimming pools to satisfy a thousand elephants are found in every school.

Personal hygiene

By use of the "New Math" master chef Pierre (Chuck) Danuel was able to calculate that the length of spaghetti needed in a chicken pie was the square of a potato equalling the hypothesis of the other two sides.

Although inedible, the judges agreed that it was the finest looking chicken pie that had been seen in international competition.

Canadians' preoccupation with soap and water is astonishing.

They shower when they get up and bath when they go down.

Why?

71

Body Odour!
A malady so terrible that even one's best friend refuses to discuss the complaint with the "complaintee".
What is B.O.?
In a nutshell it's a pong, stink, smell, stench, fetidness, fustiness or foulness emitted from the body.
The sufferer becomes flustered in the presence of superior beings.

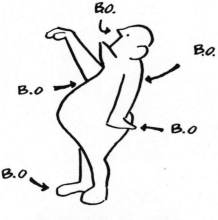

DANGER ZONES

Common to those of foreign extraction.
Do the English have B.O.?
NEVER!

Do Canadians speak English? No.

Canadians speak two languages.
One is a kind of French and the other a sort of American.
Constantly aware of the difficulties they have in being understood, the American-sounding ones reassure each other at regular intervals.
They abbreviate the words "do you understand?" and whittle it down to the phrase "eh?".
This rhymes with "day" and is used in the following manner.
"This is my new wife, eh?"
"I just bought a new car, eh?"
As to the French spoken here, I am told it's sometimes similar to that spoken across the channel.
Canada boasts of its two languages; but of what use is two if neither is English?

Can they be taught to speak English?

Yes, but it will not be easy.

The extreme weather conditions in Canada have given the Canadian mouth a permanent twist. This, coupled with a tongue that is forked (as any Indian will tell you), makes the task almost impossible.
Unfortunately Canadians have grown accustomed to their means of communication and fail to notice that they have a problem. Much of the blame for this must be laid at the door of the Canadian Broadcasting Corporation.
Started by a Canadian with a speech impediment, the company continues to this day to hire people who have voices which sound just like the voice of their founder.

ENGLISH TONGUE

FOREIGN TONGUE

Behind the Scenes
"This ... Is ... The ... Canadian ... Broadcasting ... Corporation ...," say the six
CBC announcers needed for the job as each takes a word under the direction
of the chief announcer for the day.

During the years of radio, Canadians were under the impression that this same Canadian was used for all required speech throughout the CBC.

"He don't sound like much, but look at the money we're saving," said the Canadian taxpayer.

This worked fine until the advent of television.

Now for the first time the "gaff was blown."

HERE IS THE NEWS, EH?

Canadians could see that far from being the same person reading the news or selling a car, it was in fact 6,000 readers ... and that was just in Toronto. Canadians to this day feel that it is the same voice, but laid over a different face.

Here then is the problem.
This form of hypnotic tone has deeply penetrated the subconscious of the average Canadian.
Can we correct the sound?
We can and must.
Where do we start?
English conversation classes.

A.E.I.O.U.

English conversational classes

Where can these be conducted?
The laundromat is one place that readily comes to mind.
Why the laundromat?
Because it is here that Canadians communicate with fellow Canadians.
At all other times they are too busy watching American television.
Those not at home watching American television are at the movies watching American movies.
Those unable to get in are crossing the street to the many bars.
Here they can watch American singers.
No ... the laundromat remains the ideal spot.

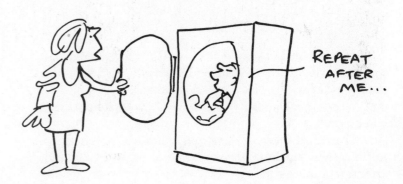

REPEAT AFTER ME...

How will we tackle the problem?
Immersion.
Complete immersion in the ways and speech of the English.
Hence, the obvious place to begin will be the outside of the laundromat.
Names such as "The Windsor Castle Scrub and Rub", or "The Britannia Wash and Dry" could be adopted.
The moment a customer enters he must feel that he is in England.

A sound system can play records of Sir Laurence Olivier and Richard Burton in selected readings.
Each washer will have a built-in speaker.
At the end of each wash "God Save Our Gracious Queen" will be played.
At this time all those in the store, regardless of whether or not it is their machine playing, will be required to stand at attention and sing along.

At the end of the rendering, three rousing cheers will be given, led by whoever's machine happens to be the one playing at that moment.
Certain disgusting habits will not be allowed to continue:
The flaunting of undies taken to and from the machines will not be tolerated. Antistatic agents must be employed to end the frantic clinging together of his and hers underwear; panty hose stuck like mad to the back of business shirts; and men's socks curled inside flimsy negligees.

Talking during the "selected readings" will not be allowed. The opening of the door to get an extra rendering of the "Queen" is strictly forbidden.

Can Canadians make it?
They must!
For them to continue in a world of "eh?" can only retard their hopes for the future.

What do Canadians do in their spare time?

Escape.
Escape from what?
Escape from their problems.
What problems? Crime for one.
Crime has increased to such an extent that to walk in the prison yard is to invite a mugging in the doorway of the warden's office.
Lights-out now finds the guards leaping into cells to take cover from sex-starved prisoners.

The churches are empty and cabins are full as Canadians beat a fast retreat with a drink in each hand and a steering wheel in the other.
Many get lost in television land.
Nightly they sit and watch as kitchen floors the size of city blocks glitter and shine at the bidding of an apron-clad sex-goddess.

Do they want a kitchen floor the size of a kitchen floor?
The women may; the men don't.
The man craves the one who's pushing the mop.

Sex

The English, being true gentlemen, do not enjoy sex.
The Canadian absolutely wallows in the stuff.

Willing girls abound in the most unlikely of places.
Seeking muscle relaxation in a massage parlor can invite an
orgy that would drive an Eastern sheik into the cold shower
before he had time to remove his glasses.

Anxious to know the positions needed to induce the magic
words "For C'rist sake, enough already!" he leaps to sex
books for the ready-made answers.
Does this mean there's a shortage of the "real" thing?
Not on your nelly!

Anxious to complete a full and accurate report, I myself visited one of these establishments.

"Starvin' Marvin's" in Toronto, despite its name, does not serve meals. It sits on the famous Street of Yonge and waits for those in need of a body rub.

What was the outside like?

This is difficult to say. I'd waited for dark before going up a poorly lit flight of stairs.

"One please."

I'd said it before I realized. This was *not* a movie house.

The girl smiled.

She was extremely attractive.

Maybe I should have said "Two please," I thought.

The waiting room was fairly full.

All were men and all had found a spot on the floor that commanded their fullest attention.

I followed the young girl down a narrow hallway.

"Which room would you like?" she asked.

"Any room will do," I mumbled.

"Well would you like France, Africa, Hong Kong or London?"

For the first time I glanced into the cubicles.

Each had wallpaper depicting a certain scene.

"I'll take Africa."

Somehow the thought of being caught in a police raid while surrounded by lions and tigers appeared more decent than being caught naked at the feet of a group of Can-Can girls.

"Wait here please."

She left the door open.

Afraid that someone might pass who knew me, I gently pushed it closed.

The room was small.

A white sheet covered the kind of table used for doctors' examinations.
I sat on the edge and began to swing my legs.
Should I undress?
Better not.
I thought again of a police raid.

The door suddenly opened.
"Hi! I'm Michelle."
"Hi! I'm ..." I began and stopped.
 Michelle had begun to remove her clothes. Whatever else she may be she was certainly not short of food at home.
"What did you say your name was?"
"Ben ..." I answered.
"O.k., Ben. Would you like to hang your scarf, overcoat, shirt, trousers and socks over there and put your dark glasses on the table?"

I wondered if I should ask her to leave the room first.
I decided against it.
There was an uncomfortable silence for ten minutes as Michelle sat on the edge of the table.
"First time?" she asked, as I finally removed my scarf.
"Yes."
She began to help.
 Appalled, I reminded her that I was an Englishman.
"Does that mean you want something extra?"
"Well, I would like a nice cup of tea," I replied.
 Maybe it was my accent. Whatever it was she was laughing so hard as she left the room that she forgot her clothes.
I waited fifteen minutes and when she failed to return I replaced my scarf and dark glasses and quietly crept away into the night.

The married Canadian

Is there such a thing as marriage in Canada?
There is; but Canadians don't know it.
Marriage for a Canadian is "til boredom do us part."
Why?
Many blame television.
Shows such as "Upstairs Downstairs" have given the Canadian women the opportunity to observe an Englishman at close quarters.

Naturally they are no longer content with their Canadian partner.
Anxious to rid themselves of their burden, Canadian women refuse to make love to their husbands.

Blaming their mates for not being English they strike back by saying "No" as a punishing act.
Look at this poor sod:

Last year Clarence was turned aside by his wife 365 times for the following reasons:

We'll wake the children .... 11 times

Pretending to sleep .... 18 times

I have a headache .... 7 times
and a record 314 times of "is that all you ever think of?"
Is it any wonder that the divorce rate in Canada is growing?

SEX WITH AN ENGLISHMAN

LONGING

PASSION

INTERCOURSE

SATISFACTION

SEX WITH A CANADIAN

LONGING

PASSION

INTERCOURSE

SATISFACTION

Sport

There are certain games played by Canadians; but these are as far removed from being involved in sport as an Englishman is from being involved in sex.
There is something called ice-hockey that surely takes the biscuit.

Ice-hockey

The game consists of two teams:
Players and non-players.
Those on the players' team wear ice-skates.
Those on the non-players wear scowls and walk up and down behind those wearing skates.
All those participating in the game are enclosed in two small boxes.
These boxes are placed at the edge of a large area of ice.
The position of these boxes is extremely important.

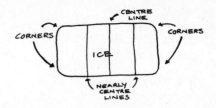

Both of these boxes must face each other and are linked by a line that runs across the ice surface.
Why the line?
This enables the paying customers to find their team.
Many still have difficulty but are quickly shown who's who by fellow Canadians who seem to be only too pleased to throw an object of some sort in the direction of a team member.

Each of the two boxes have a door.
These doors are used for coming in from the ice surface – but never for going out onto the ice.
At irregular intervals players leap from the boxes, charge the nearest player to them, and immediately skate toward a smaller box assisted by an official wearing a striped shirt.

The moment the player is in the smaller box, the non-players stop walking up and down and begin to swear and point.

Meanwhile the ones wearing ice skates begin to remove their clothing and dance with each other.

In the larger and more affluent buildings music is provided by an organist whose repertoire consists of one song played in little snippets throughout the evening.

A small black object called a puck is involved too, but appears to be of little importance.

Scoring?

I haven't the faintest idea. . . .

Being English I have found better things to do with my time at 8 p.m. on a Saturday night.

Football

The Canadian game of *foot*ball is played by picking the ball up and throwing it to a fellow who catches it.

A number of large men wear numbers on their backs.

These numbers are extremely important.

Once the game begins it is only by hearing his number called that a team member knows that he is about to be carried from the field on a stretcher.

Art

A member of the Group of Seven, Franklin Carmichael, hides his face as he paints La Cloche Mountain, Grace Lake, circa 1931.

Art in Canada is the "Group of Seven."

Who are the Group of Seven and why are these the only paintings sold?

To find the answer to these questions we must start at the beginning.

The first thing we learn is that the Group of Seven were originally 189 strong.

The year was 1887.

Settlers were arriving in Canada by the bucketfull.

Most of them were farmers, carpenters and politicians.

The politicians, anxious to have their achievements recorded, approached the carpenters to paint their pictures.

"Are you akidding, man? (Most were European.)

We gotta build the loga cabins for yous guys."

So it fell to the lot of the farmers.
These men of the fields began to paint in their spare time.
All of their work remains to this day, unsold.
Why?
Being farmers they used a roller.
Who paints a picture with a roller?
Who said anything about pictures!
They were painting their barns.

Annoyed at having spent so much money on boxes of oil paints only to have them end up on the sides of barns, the politicians recalled all paint boxes.
The farmers, who by now had begun to enjoy painting, decided to try and hold onto their oil colours.
In a last ditch attempt to impress the politicians they headed for the woods.
Only 189 made it.

The others were caught before they could take the top off the turpentine and were forced to hand over their art supplies.
Of the 189 who made it, all without exception found refuge in northern Ontario.

There they began to paint trees.
Finding it difficult to paint leaves, you can imagine their delight when they found a tree that had lost most of its leaves.
With one whoop they leaped to the tree.
One hundred and eighty-nine brushes slapped the canvas.
Arguments developed. One wanted the green paint as another was about to paint a leaf.
Then fights began. ...
In no time at all just seven remained of the original 189 painters.

Meanwhile the tree had taken a tremendous amount of pushing and shoving during the fights that had taken place around its trunk.

It now leaned toward the lake.

Obviously there was an angle that showed the tree to its best advantage. No-one was going to buy a painting of a tree that looked half-dead.

Soon all seven painters were trying to use the same spot from which to paint.

Too late they found that the tree was cursed.

One by one the seven began to die.

One was accidently hit by a canoe that the others held above his head as he reached for the burnt umber.

Another sat on a paint brush that had been left on his stool in an upright position and died of lead poisoning.

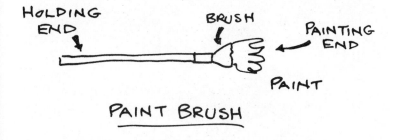

Now just two of the original 189 remain.

Canadian artist Frank Charles lifts his easel in a desperate attempt to ward off an attack by William Jones who is after the red paint. Meanwhile, Harold Evans, a Canadian painter famous for his painting "Snow in the summer of '89", attempts to hold back Mrs. Charles.

An interesting pose can be seen to the left of the picture. This is Teddy Adams, another of the Group of 189. Seconds before this picture was taken Adams had been stabbed.

For those interested in the technical details:
the brush was a Windsor Newton: No. 2 series 7: sable.

Harold Town, lives in Toronto and paints pictures that no-one understands and everyone buys fearing that to refuse will be to encourage the curse of the "Lakeshore Tree."

The Tree far away

A.Y. Jackson
Night, Georgian Bay   1913
(National Gallery)

The Tree closer

A. J. Casson
White Pine   1957
(McMichael Collection)

The Tree close-up

Tom Thomson
The Jack Pine   1917
(National Gallery)

Canadian music

Anne Murray is Canadian music.
A school teacher who always wanted to make money,
Anne was skipping home across the mountains of Halifax
when she was spotted by an American film director.
The rest is history.

Other Canadians have made it to the big time in music but
they are few in number:

Glen Gould	Sam The Record Man
Mareen Forester	Betty Kennedy and
Gordon Lightfoot	Gordon Sinclair.

THE HILLS ARE ALIVE, WITH THE — SOUND OF MUSIC

American singing star Donny Osmond made a surprise visit to Director Ben Wicks' headquarters in Toronto and challenged Wicks on his "English are best" theory.

Beaten by pure logic, Osmond switched tactics and tried to fight back by challenging Wicks to a teeth contest.

Flashing a group of 14 uncapped uppers and lowers, Osmond was stunned to find a group of unmarked 15 zinging back at him.

Before leaving the area of Canadian music I am compelled to mention Canada's greatest hit of all time.
It remains a study piece for people throughout the world who are struggling to overcome what has been diagnosed as
a "learning disability":

O Canada

Our home and native land

True patriot love

In all thy son's command

With glowing hearts

We see thee rise

The true north strong and free

And stand on guard

O Canada

We stand on guard for thee.

O Canada

Glorious and free

O Canada

We stand on guard for thee

O Canada

We stand on guard for thee.

Do Canadians work?

Very few.

Conscious that the way to beat inflation was to encourage restraint, the Canadian government set up a committee. The findings of this committee were published in 1975. They discovered that an unemployed person used more restraint and spent less money than he did when he was employed.

Since this discovery, the government has persuaded as many people as possible to leave their jobs.

The programme has enjoyed a tremendous success.

Last winter almost 500,000 Canadians took advantage of the government's scheme.

"With luck," one government official told me, "we'll have everyone out by next Christmas."

Will the English settlers be required to work?

Certainly not.

As a member of the aristocracy you will be exempt. Naturally!

Canadians are so anxious to have the English aristocrats live amongst them that they will certainly not wish to tire these gentlemen out with something as uncouth as manual labour.

However, Canadians may come forward and ask for advice during a strike period.

This is only to be expected in view of the past successes that Englishmen have had in the putting down of native unrest in the colonies.

What about the English who already live in Canada?

Most of them can be seen mixing freely with Canadians from all walks of life.

They are the working or "lower" class and Canada is full of them.

Success for them has been membership in a North American union.

In keeping with their British habit these same workers have carried their ability to "stop work at the drop of a hat" into their new surroundings.

Even Canadians now feel that they have more than enough of "that" kind of Englishman.

No, what Canada needs now is an army of aristocrats.

Men who have never walked out on a job, for the simple reason that they have never had a job.

The Canadian home

The Englishman's home is his castle.
The Canadian's home is on the range.

Despite this fact, a trait common with most Canadians is that he insists in showing a visitor around his house: Before you've had time to take your hand off the doorknob a voice is asking "Would you like the grand tour?"

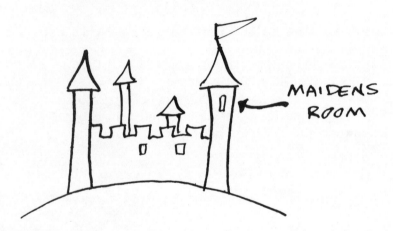

ENGLISH
HOME

CANADIAN
HOME

Try to refuse.

The less seen of a Canadian home the better.

Certainly to see a Canadian bathroom for the first time can be a traumatic experience.

In England the toilet is correctly placed in a room of its own. Here in Canada you will notice that the toilet sits in all its ugliness beside the bathtub!

Unlike the Canadian bathroom that boasts a "toilet", the English insist on other extras when cleansing themselves.

Your reaction will no doubt follow mine.

Before I took my first Canadian bath I placed a chair behind the door feeling sure that a stranger might enter to use the toilet as I looked on helplessly from a sea of bubbles.

Avoid the tour.
Continue on into the living room and sit amongst the collection of hideous pine furniture and fake antiques that hide behind the curtains of most Canadian homes.

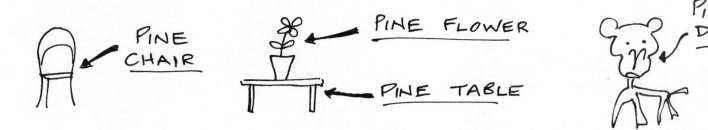

Once seated in the house you'll be expected to talk ("Oh I just love the way he talks, don't you Chuck?").
Unlike an Englishman's conversation, much of what the Canadian talks about is related to a lot of boring rubbish concerning life in North America.

Boring Canadian	Bright and Breezy English
Canadian Weather	English Weather
Canadian Cars	English Cars
Canadian Culture	English Culture
Canadian Schools	English Schools
Canadian Children	English Children
Dieppe	El Alamein
Sex	Cricket

Self-control

Excited at the thought of an Englishman in the house most Canadians lose complete control of themselves.

IT'S AN ENGLISHMAN!

It's an important occasion for them and, as happens on most important occasions, accidents will occur.
The most likely of these will be related to some disgusting personal problem.

The English, of course, have perfect manners.
The Canadian, however, appears to have little or no control over a certain unpleasant body function.
Rather than move away from the affected area they will take you by the arm and continue their conversation making it impossible to escape.

Unlike the English girl who detracts attention from the accident ("Look there! Isn't that a squirrel?") the Canadian will scrape her foot on the floor in a clumsy attempt to shift the blame.

During a recent visit to Canada, Sir Ian Packard was forced to call the police. Bertha Roads of Moose Jaw was so excited at the thought of an Englishman's visit that she was unable to control her feelings.

"I tried to make it a quiet one," explained the embarrassed Bertha. Sir Ian agreed to drop all charges after he'd been given a new shirt.

Sickness

Doctors in Canada are paid an incredible amount of money.
Embarrassed at this they feel obligated to do more than what is expected of them.

Entering a hospital in Canada with a chill, one is liable to leave minus a spleen, liver and tonsils. Added to which your ears have been syringed, hair parted, teeth cleaned and a bungled vasectomy straightened.

The Canadian doctor is so happy in his work that it is with great difficulty he is persuaded to stop. Even in the bath a small buzzer attached to his lower lip will signal the time and place of another victim.
They are vehemently opposed to two things:
Other opinions and house calls.

WHICH LEG
WOULD
YOU LIKE
REMOVED
NEXT ?

Death

Death for the Canadian is horror.

Unlike the English who speak of "a nice way to go" or the Irish wake in the form of a glorious piss-up, the Canadian is appalled at the thought of a lonely eternity.

To the very last he wants the lid of his coffin up so that he can relish the gaze of his mates as they silently parade past his "laid-out" form.

Not content with this, all car lights are then turned on in a last show of togetherness as the group heads off toward that great resting place in the sky.

Canada's past

Unfortunately there is little of it.
And what there is remains a bore.
The one fact that you will need to know is how Canada became one nation.
She built a railroad.

Or to be more precise a Mr. Pierre Berton built a railroad. Tired of his job as a newspaperman Mr. Berton decided to write a book.

Having always wanted to be an engine driver he decided that his book would be about trains.
To his astonishment he found that most Canadians did not know what a railroad was.
Anxious to attract as many travellers as he could (and so give him the material for his book), Mr. Berton decided to build a railroad that would link both coasts.

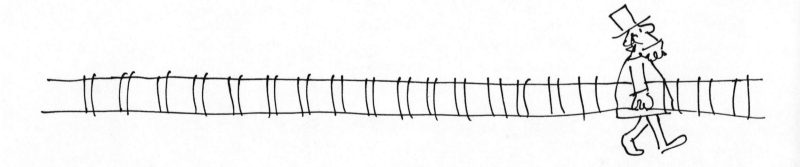

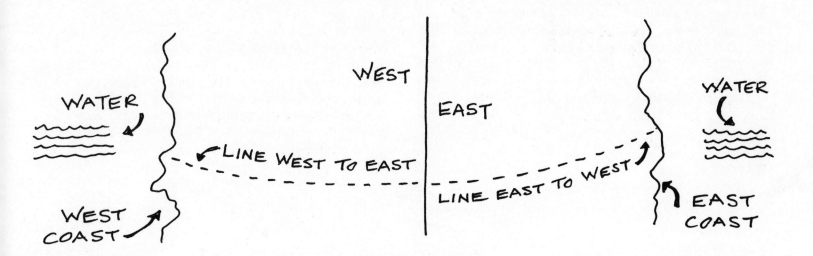

WATER

WEST

EAST

WATER

LINE WEST TO EAST

LINE EAST TO WEST

WEST COAST

EAST COAST

Not wishing to show favouritism it was decided to build two railway lines.
One from East to West and one from West to East.
Unable to spell the word Canadian it was agreed by Mr. Berton that the lines would be known as C.P. and C.N.

IT COMES AFTER 'B', PIERRE!

Naturally such an undertaking was a tremendous task. Although capable of most things it became quite apparent that Mr Berton would need assistance.

Being seven-foot-six in height and fearing the ridicule that would be heaped upon him if he were photographed with smaller men, Mr Berton set off in search of tall help.

Unfortunately such help was not available. So he decided on an obvious solution.

Men of average height wearing tall hats.

Conscious of the embarrassment of being seen in public wearing such ridiculous hats most of the workers took to growing beards as a disguise.

Men of average height wearing tall hats seen here giving Mr. Berton much needed help.

So they began.

One group laying rails from the Pacific coast and one group laying rails from the Atlantic coast.

Their plan was to meet in the centre of the Rockies.

Here, if a mistake were made, it would be possible to cover the error with a tunnel.

Unfortunately many of the workers followed the lead of their Prime Minister and began to have a drink during their lunch hour.

As a direct result the meeting of the rail-line that had been planned for tunnel mountain did in point of fact fail to materialize.

Missing by something like four feet, both lines passed each other and continued on to their respective opposite coasts.

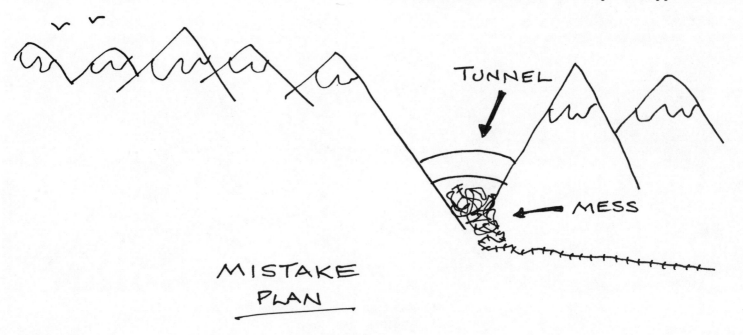

TUNNEL

MESS

MISTAKE
PLAN

Not wishing to start again it was decided that each group
would turn and try again.
This they did.
For this reason there are two rail-lines crossing Canada.

Odds and ends about Canada

The cocktail party

Don't ring the bell.
Walk right in.
The hallway will be crowded with people you have never seen before.
One will take you by the hand.
Friendly?
Not at all.
This guest will be attempting to get into a pair of someone else's overshoes.
They need you for support as they stand on one leg.

Don't be surprised if the same person thanks you for a delightful evening as you hold the door open for them to leave.
Head straight for the kitchen.
Why the kitchen?
This is where most of the guests will be standing watching the booze that they have brought with them. To leave the kitchen will be to allow a guest who has not brought booze to have a go at yours.

After a few belts, make your way to the living room.

A person will be circulating with drinks on a silver tray.

It's the remains of the punch made by the man of the house for the previous party.

Grab one.

Only when a person has a drink in his hand is he allowed to converse.

The first Canadian you meet will ask,

"And what do you do?"

This is an old Canadian custom and roughly translated means:

(A) Are you in a job that could do me some good?

(B) Are you in a job that could do my son some good?

(C) Are you in a job?

The question is asked as the person asking it looks over your shoulder.

A good trick is to make sure the glass you are holding is nearly empty before trying this question on someone.

Should the answer to your question

"And what do you do?" be "Me? I'm an economics professor," it's possible to finish the drink in one gulp and answer

"Wonderful. Excuse me. Just off for a refill. Stay right there. I'll be right back."

The "stay right there" is extremely important.

No point in escaping to the kitchen to find the same economics professor by your right elbow again.

A good place to hide is the "loo" or as it's known here, the bathroom.

Unfortunately it's probably occupied.

Canadians use the bathroom almost as much as they use the television.

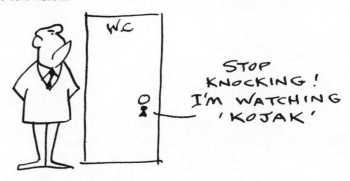

Naturally as the evening progresses it will not be necessary to make excuses when faced with a boring drinking companion. You can be blunt.

Most Canadians answer with their favourite repartee, "Don't give me that shit!"

The first meeting you will have with the host will be as you are about to head for a real cracker who is sitting alone and has been giving you the "have you seen upstairs yet?" look.

CAN YOU DIRECT ME UPSTAIRS?

Within two paces of this gem the host will grab your hands and shout

"I want you to meet someone!"

The person they have in mind is the ugliest person you have ever seen and will be an expert on Canadian poets.

"This is Marion. She writes and is dying to meet you."

Food will be served long after you need it.

In this way most Canadians keep their budget for parties to the minimum, finding that the booze that the guests bring is cheaper than the food they themselves must buy.

For them a guy under the couch is worth two at the table.

YOUR FLY IS OPEN!

When the food does arrive you will be asked to serve yourself and find a seat.

This can be tricky.

You are now standing in the centre of the room watching the cracker go upstairs with a most unattractive man, as you have in your hand a scotch, bowl of salad, glass of wine, roll and butter, cup of coffee, some ham and fiddleheads. In your right hand you will have the salt and pepper for the girl who is standing beside you speaking about a Canadian poet who lives in Regina.

When you leave, thank the person who has given the party. She will be the one you have seen the least during the evening and can be found at the kitchen sink washing the dishes to save herself the job in the morning.

GOODNIGHT
AND
THANKS FOR
COMING!

On the bus

Since an English gentleman would rather be seen inside a coffin than inside a bus, this may seem like an unnecessary piece of informantion.

However it can be fun ... just once.

Most Canadian buses are of the one-level variety.

Unfortunately Canadian technology has not progressed to the stage where the placing of an "upstairs" on a bus is deemed safe.

Although the first experimental model test-driven in Winnipeg succeeded in turning the corner at a street called Portage, the top failed to make the turn and continued on down Main Street (see photograph).

The top section of an experimental double-decked street car finally stopped four blocks from where the bottom section has made a turn. In this rare Winnipeg photograph relatives and friends can be seen rushing forward to help those still trapped in the upper section.

There are two doors on most buses found in Canada. This enables those getting on the front of the bus to block the path of those attempting to get off the rear.

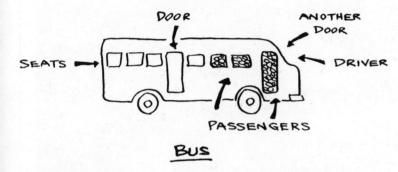

BUS

Canadians do not queue (or "line-up" as they say in Canada) for a bus. They much prefer to conduct themselves in an animal-like manner and elbow their way past those of smaller stature.
This is why I strongly advise the carrying of a brolly.
A sharp tap on the head followed by the expletive, "Who the hell do you think you're pushing?" works wonders, although I did have reason to be speechless when one Canadian turned and replied:
"I don't know. What's your name?"
Once the bus arrives step smartly aboard, drop the required fare into a small container, and take a seat.

This can be difficult during rush hour but can be accomplished by pushing a slower or older person to one side. Should they fail to move, a swift punch in the kidneys will show them that you are not to be taken lightly. On sitting, immediately open your newspaper and cover the face.

CORRECT WAY TO COVER FACE   INCORRECT

This should bar your line of vision if a cripple or pregnant woman get on at the next stop.
The driver on Canadian buses works without the help of a conductor. He is required to count money, give tickets, direct passengers, call out street names, and occasionally start the bus without throwing all standing passengers to the floor.

In the cab

We know it as a taxi.
Here in Canada it's possible to sit with the driver.
Why anyone would want to be seen sitting with the driver?
Damned if I know.
I suspect it's another example of this "classless" society that the natives are constantly yapping about.

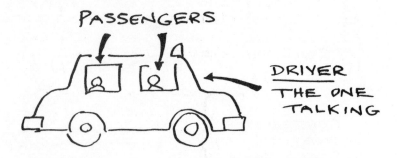

The back seats of all cabs contain a photograph of the driver. This is to enable you to point him out in a future police line-up should you find yourself unwittingly involved in a bank hold-up in which your cab was used as the getaway vehicle.

The price charged for your journey is shown on a small meter beside the driver. However this amount should in no way be taken as the amount of money that the driver expects to be paid.
He will expect more.
Unlike the London driver who will ask with a scream, "Wot the hell do yer call this?"
the Canadian cab-driver will smile sweetly and gently squeeze you and your pockets against the nearest brick wall.

Riding a bike

By far the most popular of Canadian pastimes is to own a bicycle.

This means of keeping fit can be leaned up against the garage wall gathering dust.

Why?

Because to ride them can be extremely dangerous.

Roads in Canada are for *cars*:

Any other vehicle is quickly flattened (with the exception of a truck).

Providing for the Canadian needs, many provincial governments decided to build biking paths....

These are used for jogging.

Jogging

Nobody wishes to be pointed out as the most grotesque looking flabby-bellied creature ever seen.

Determined Canadians either jog extremely early in the morning or extremely late at night.

All those taking part wear track suits.

This is a garment that covers any likely dollops of skin that other garments would release to all and sundry.

These Canadians jog for 20 minutes a day during one two-week period.

They then come to their senses and quit.

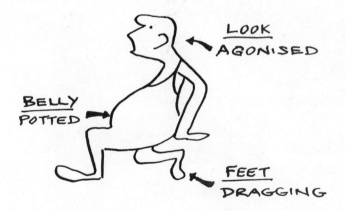

LOOK AGONISED

BELLY POTTED

FEET DRAGGING

This, then, is Canada.
Will there be room for our English saviours?
We must make room!

Finding room: the basic plan

Two Canadians, obviously anxious to get a choice lot, argue as to who was the first on the particular spot they have chosen for their new home.

Obviously any plan for foreigners must be kept simple. Condescendingly, I have opted for something uncomplicated. . . .

Everyone in Canada will be asked to move 450 miles north.

Most Canadians can walk in a straight line and have an uncanny knack of knowing the direction of North.
Some will protest: for instance those who are happiest living in their present homes. (Many of these will be in the upper-income bracket.) Unfortunately their homes are the ones most suited to our needs.

It will not be easy for them to give up their mansion-style living.
Will they understand?
I am sure they will.
We will explain that a first-class person will not fit into a second-class home,
that cream will not mix with water,
that here is an opportunity for Canada to reseed,
a means of replacing the weeds with flowers. ...

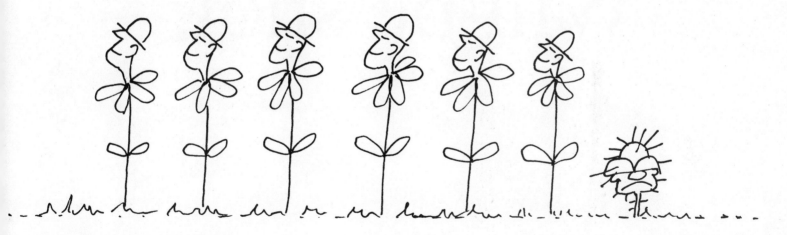

Who could resist such an argument?
Those who refuse ...

Will be shot.

What will be done with the politicians?

These will be allowed to remain in the south.
Accustomed as they are to mingling with the dignitaries and others in the upper-class of other countries, they will be ideally suited for their new role: servants to the English arrivals.

Groomed in Canada's best schools they should quickly adapt to the new role of supplying the needs of an English gentleman.
Naturally there will be problems.
Their past has been filled with the pretence of carrying out the wishes of others. Continuance of this pretence in the presence of English gentry will not be tolerated.
I myself would favour getting Mr. Trudeau.
Would this be possible?
It's my understanding that he has a good mind and could pass away many a long winter evening regaling me with stories of his travels. He also speaks French, which could be good fun and a relief from the North American accent.

SHALL I RUN YOUR BATH NOW, SIR?

International support

Support for the basic plan has been overwhelming.
For some unknown reason this support has come with one
exception from those living outside of Canada.
Here are a few well-known faces and their comments.
"I think you ought to get a medal." *Michael Cain.*
"The most courageous thing I've heard of since I met Billy
Jean King." *Bobby Riggs.*
"If only you were King of Sweden, Ben." *Ingrid Bergman.*
"If I gave you my Academy Award would you let me come
with you?" *Shirley Jones.*
"It's people like you that make me proud to be a
Canadian." *John Diefenbaker.*
"Gee. It would be great to live in a country under your kind
of rule." *Yogi Berra.*
"Brilliant," *Malcolm Muggeridge.*
"Damned devilish." *David Niven.*
"You should be a general." *Colonel Saunders.*
"Dear Ben." *Dear Abby.*

Conclusion

This concludes my report.
There are many areas that I have neglected to cover.
For this, I am sorry.
Time is short.
If Englishmen are to come to Canada, they must come
N O W.
However, there is one small point I neglected to mention.

We will need a leader for this nation of future super-beings.

    He will need to be English

    Strong

    Modest

    Silent

    Handsome

    A person of superior intellect
and incredible writing skill. ...

Need I say more?
You have read this report.

I accept, in all humbleness.

And now, if you will.
Place your hands to your sides.
Feet together.
Chin in.
Chest out (for those with chests).
Back straight.
Heads up.
Mouth open wide and all together ...

God save our gracious Queen,
Long live our noble Queen
God save our Queen.
Send her victorious
Happy and glorious
Long to reign over us
God save our Queen.